The Blessing Cup

The Blessing Cup: PRAYER-RITUALS FOR FAMILIES AND GROUPS

ROCK TRAVNIKAR, O.F.M.

ST. ANTHONY MESSENGER PRESS

Cincinnati, Ohio

Nihil Obstat: Rev. Thomas Richstatter, O.F.M.
Rev. Robert A. Stricker
Rev. Edward J. Gratsch

Imprimi Potest: Rev. Fred Link, O.F.M.
Provincial
Rev. John Bok, O.F.M.
Provincial

Imprimatur: +Most Reverend Carol K. Moeddel
Vicar General and Auxiliary Bishop
Archdiocese of Cincinnati
December 14, 1993
January 22, 2002

Scripture citations are taken from *The New Revised Standard Version Bible*, copyright ©1989 by the Division of Christian Education of the National Council of Churches of Christ in the United States of America, and used by permission. All rights reserved.

Cover and interior design by Mark Sullivan
Illustrations by Julie Lonneman
Cover photo by Daniel Fox
Blessing cup by Follette Pottery, phone: 318.251.1310

Library of Congress Cataloging-in-Publication Data

Travnikar, Rock.
  The blessing cup : prayer-rituals for families and groups / Rock Travnikar.— [Rev. and expanded ed.].
     p. cm.
  ISBN 0-86716-486-7 (pbk.)
  1. Family—Prayer-books and devotions—English. 2. Catholic Church—Prayer-books and devotions—English. I. Title.
  BX2170.F3 T73 2002
  249—dc21
                                        2002003199
ISBN 0-86716-486-7

Published by St. Anthony Messenger Press
www.AmericanCatholic.org
Printed in the U.S.A

With gratitude I dedicate this book to my parents,
JOSEPH AND CAROLINE TRAVNIKAR.
Their example and the blessing they gave me
in a home of joyful sons and daughters
is the blessing I offer all the families
who make the blessing cup a part of their tradition.

TABLE OF CONTENTS

FOREWORD

Back in 1979, when I was a brand-new book editor at St. Anthony Messenger Press, one of the first manuscripts entrusted to my care was a delightful little book called *The Blessing Cup: 24 Simple Rites for Family Prayer-Celebrations*. Adapted from *Little Liturgies for Christian Families* by the Lutheran pastor Jack W. Lundin, it was Father Rock's first venture into publishing. Together we looked forward to its arrival from the printer with all the eagerness of first-time parents. We even had a fond nickname for the "baby": "Blessy."

Over the years, "Blessy" has done what babies do best: It has grown. Its first revision in 1993 contained forty blessing prayers. Now that it has reached adulthood, it has grown in both size and popularity. This latest edition contains twenty-eight new blessings to help families and groups bring their concerns to God in times of joy and excitement, in times of stress and sorrow.

My four children were all in their teens when the first edition appeared; now I enjoy a wealth of grandchildren. One conviction I hold, acquired long before I met Father Rock, is that ritual is a powerful binding force. From the bedtime routines toddlers insist upon to the comic routines that leave outsiders puzzled, all groups, including families, shape their identity by the rites they observe. And, in the process, they discover that something holy lies at the heart of their relationships.

It is that sense of the holy that these prayers are designed to bring into focus, for gatherings of believing people claim a deeper identity as God's people. Those who share the eucharistic cup know that, in Jesus, nothing human is undeserving of God's attention, that God rejoices with us when we are happy and sorrows with us when troubles come our way.

For nearly a quarter of a century now, families and other groups have honed their sense of God's nearness with this book. May its latest revision bring your family or group ever closer, bound by the love God has poured out on all of us. My own experience convinces me that it will.

Carol Luebering

INTRODUCTION TO THE 2002 EXPANDED EDITION

Tumbling down a hill, a snowball grows. *The Blessing Cup* has grown as it has been used by people near and far. Base Christian communities, family gatherings and folks met along the way have offered suggestions and given their support and encouragement. It is my prayer that more and more people will use this book as a launchpad for their own blessings. The cup is made holy by those who gather around it, and the best rites for family or group prayer-celebrations are written first in your heart.

The Blessing Cup first appeared in 1979. The first edition contained, as its subtitle stated, "twenty-four simple rites for family prayer-celebrations." These prayers were inspired by the people of St. Agnes Church in Dayton, Ohio, and the Knightswood and Belle Vista neighborhood groups of St. Therese Church in Fort Wayne, Indiana.

Additional services for the revised edition and for this expanded edition of *The Blessing Cup* were inspired by many readers and commentators along the way. Certainly, the community of believers at Mother of Good Counsel Catholic Community of Hazard, Kentucky, with retreatants of Lumen Christi in the Diocese of Houma-Thibodaux, Louisiana, have influenced these additions. I wish to offer my personal gratitude to St. Anthony Messenger Press, to editor April Bolton, Sister Janet Schneider, C.D.P., and Jennifer Landry for their support and encouragement. It is my hope that these sixty-eight services will be but a springboard to the creative development of your own family's prayer.

Groups or families who are striving to strengthen bonds do so by mutually sharing hopes and fears, joys and sorrows. The blessing cup is a tradition you can begin in your home or meeting place to help you toward this goal.

Used as a family or group symbol, the blessing cup can become a sign of solidarity—oneness in prayer and blessing. The blessing cup service, centered around a common cup and based on the use of Scripture and petition, can help family or group members express their deepest feelings.

So select a cup—metal, pottery or glass. Keep it in a prominent place to remind you of your mutual hope. Then gather your family or group for prayer at special times—holidays, birthdays, anniversaries, times of change, growth or loss.

Before beginning your celebration, decide who will lead the prayer and who will read the Scriptures. These might be permanent responsibilities; in a growing family it is more likely that roles will become more flexible as the family matures. In a small group, members come and go, so the role of leader will need to be flexible, too.

Let the filling of the cup be a ceremonious act—even a special privilege—that marks the beginning of a special event. Fill it with your favorite beverage—whatever fits the occasion and the taste of the participants. Then open the prayer with the Sign of the Cross, presenting the significance of the day to the Lord in a few words. Listen together to a brief passage from Scripture that relates to the event you celebrate.

The leader can then announce the response to the petitions and start them with a few prayers formulated in advance. Other family or group members are then invited to add their particular prayers—perhaps a special birthday wish or a particular worry—or are left free to pray silently for needs that words refuse to hold.

When the leader senses that all have had their say, he or she collects the family's or group's prayers into one, the "collect," and offers them to the Lord.

The unity achieved in prayer is then celebrated by passing the common cup.

A prayer or song lifted in unison, perhaps with hands held around the family or group circle, seals the individual members as one before the Lord, and the simple ritual is ended.

May your blessing cup be filled to overflowing!

Family Life

"Child, why have you treated us like this? Look, your father and I have been searching for you in great anxiety." He said to them, "Why were you searching for me? Did you not know that I must be in my Father's house?" But they did not understand what he said to them. Then he went down with them and came to Nazareth, and was obedient to them. His mother treasured all these things in her heart.

(Luke 2:48–52)

Dedication of the Family Blessing Cup

Opening Prayer

Loving God, we ask your blessing on us all as we dedicate this cup together, in the name of the Father, and of the Son, and of the Holy Spirit.

Scripture

The cup of blessing that we bless, is it not a sharing in the blood of Christ? (1 Corinthians 10:16a)

Petitions

May this cup symbolize our love for each other, Lord, we pray.
Response: Bless us, Lord.
May it represent a shared love that grows by your grace each day, Lord, we pray.
May it be a sign of the trust that we have in you and in each other, Lord, we pray.
May we willingly share our hopes, dreams and fears, our joys and disappointments around our family cup of blessing, Lord, we pray.
Add your own petitions.

Collect

Holy be this cup which we raise in blessing. May we grow in a sense of mutual family love sharing in this one cup.

Sharing of the Blessing Cup
Pray together the Our Father or sing an appropriate song.

A FAMILY PRAYER

Opening Prayer

We walk together in the light of God's blessing, in the name of the Father, and of the Son, and of the Holy Spirit.

Scripture

Then [the disciples] told what had happened on the road, and how he had been made known to them in the breaking of the bread.

While they were talking about this, Jesus himself stood among them and said to them, "Peace be with you." (Luke 24:35–36)

Petitions

May we love one another as Christ loves us, we pray.

Response: We are your family, Lord.

May we grow in our ability to see Christ in each other, we pray.

For the needs of our family and each other, we pray.

Add your own petitions.

Collect

Today, _____, _____ and _____ have spoken what is in their hearts, recognizing the journey of Christ with this family. May we always walk with Christ.

Sharing of the Blessing Cup

Pray together the Our Father or sing an appropriate song.

For the Blessing of a Home

Opening Prayer
> Bless this house, Lord, and those who live here, in the name of the Father, and of the Son, and of the Holy Spirit.

Scripture
> Unless the LORD builds the house,
> those who build it labor in vain.
> Unless the LORD guards the city,
> The guard keeps watch in vain. (Psalm 127:1)

Petitions
> We praise and thank you for _____,
> _____ and _____ who together form this household, as we ask your blessing.
> *Response:* Bless us, Lord.
> We pray that this home may be a reflection of the grace-filled home of Nazareth, blessed by Christ himself, as we ask your blessing.
> We pray that your Spirit may rest in the hearts of this family and in this home, as we ask your blessing.
> *Add your own petitions.*

Collect
> Your abundant goodness has given us cause to rejoice in this people and this place. Send your angels to watch over and to protect all who dwell in this house.

Sharing of the Blessing Cup
> *Pray together the Our Father or sing an appropriate song.*

A MEAL BLESSING I

Opening Prayer

We gather at this table united in love for one another in the name of the Father, and of the Son, and of the Holy Spirit.

Scripture

...[T]he earth is full of the steadfast love of
the LORD.
By the word of the LORD the heavens were made,
and all their host by the breath of his mouth...
Let all the earth fear the LORD;
let all the inhabitants of the world stand in awe of
him.
(Psalm 33:5b–6a, 8)

Petitions

For the bounty of this table, we are grateful, and we pray.
Response: We give you thanks.
For those who nurture us in word and deed, we pray.
For those who are gathered here this day, we pray.
Add your own petitions.

Collect

What return shall we make to the Lord for all that he has given us? We take up the cup of salvation and call on the name of the Lord.

Sharing of the Blessing Cup

Pray together the traditional meal prayer or say your own prayer of thanks as the cup is passed.

A MEAL BLESSING II

Opening Prayer

Around this table we are nourished by the gifts of Earth and Spirit in the name of the Father, and of the Son, and of the Holy Spirit.

Scripture

So Jesus sent Peter and John, saying, "Go and prepare the Passover meal for us that we may eat it." They asked him, "Where do you want us to make preparations for it?" "Listen," he said to them, "when you have entered the city, a man carrying a jar of water will meet you; follow him into the house he enters and say to the owner of the house, 'The teacher asks you, "Where is the guest room, where I may eat the Passover with my disciples?"'" He will show you a large room upstairs, already furnished. Make preparations for us there." So they went and found everything as he had told them; and they prepared the Passover meal. (Luke 22:8–12)

Petitions

Unite us in faith, family and friendship, we pray.
Response: Bless us, Lord.
Give us what we need for those who are hungry and homeless, we pray.
For those who have brought us to this table and joined us in the breaking of the bread and sharing of this cup, we pray.
Add your own petitions.

Collect

Bless us, O Lord, and these thy gifts, which we are about to receive through Christ our Lord.

Sharing of the Blessing Cup

Express your thanks as the cup is passed from one person to another at the table.

CELEBRATING A BIRTHDAY

Opening Prayer

We come together to raise our blessing cup and to celebrate the birthday of _____. We give thanks to God for the life and hope that is within _____, whose birth we celebrate, in the name of the Father, and of the Son, and of the Holy Spirit.

Scripture

For this I was born, and for this I came into the world, to testify to the truth. Everyone who belongs to the truth listens to my voice. (John 18:37b)

Petitions

With thanks to God for revealing Jesus to us through _____, we pray.
Response: Hear us, Lord.
With thanks for the love of Christ which is mirrored in the life of _____, we pray.
May _____ always be free in the spirit of Christ, we pray.
Add your own petitions.

Collect

Christ, born to redeem humankind, bless us in this celebration.

Sharing of the Blessing Cup
Pray together the Our Father or sing "Happy Birthday" or another appropriate song.

Announcing or Celebrating a Pregnancy

Opening Prayer

We are filled with gratitude as we share in God's creative goodness, in the name of the Father, and of the Son, and of the Holy Spirit.

Scripture

Elkanah knew his wife Hannah, and the LORD remembered her. In due time Hannah conceived and bore a son. She named him Samuel, for she said, "I have asked him of the LORD."
(1 Samuel 1:19b–20)

Petitions

Joyfully we await the birth of this child, as we pray.
Response: Be with us, Lord.
For health and well-being for all parents and their unborn children, we pray.
Create a space in our lives, our home and our family where this child can grow in wisdom, age and grace, we pray.
Add your own petitions.

Collect

Form and fashion us as a household that reveals the handiwork of God. In these exciting months ahead, may we be a celebration of life.

Sharing of the Blessing Cup
Pray together the Hail Mary or sing an appropriate song.

CELEBRATING FAMILY RECONCILIATION

THIS SERVICE COULD BE USED PRIOR TO A COMMUNAL PENANCE SERVICE OR IN THE RECONCILIATION OF FAMILY MEMBERS.

Opening Prayer

Lord, we have not always been the best sign of your love for us. We are sorry, and we pray in the name of the Father, and of the Son, and of the Holy Spirit.

Scripture

If we confess our sins, he who is faithful and just will forgive us our sins and cleanse us from all unrighteousness. (1 John 1:9)

Petitions

Lord, it is you who forgives us. Help us to forgive each other, we pray.
Response: Lord, have mercy.
Lord, we have forgotten your goodness. Help us to return to you, we pray.
Lord, we have failed to remember that everything we are and have is a gift from you. Forgive us, we pray.
Add your own petitions.

Collect

Lord, you have shown us how to live and forgive. For this we are filled with thanks. We will do our best to be new persons, better persons, each day. Help us to be at peace with each other and to forgive in your name.

Sharing of the Blessing Cup
   Pray together the Our Father or an act of contrition.

For a Family Reunion

THIS SERVICE MAY BE USED TO COMMEMORATE AN ANNUAL FAMILY RE-UNION. IT MAY ALSO CELEBRATE THE FINDING OF MISSING OR SEPARATED RELATIVES OR THE MEETING OF A BIRTH PARENT AND AN ADOPTED CHILD.

Opening Prayer

With praise and thanksgiving we gather together in the name of the Father, and of the Son, and of the Holy Spirit.

Scripture

Then our mouth was filled with laughter,
   and our tongue with shouts of joy;
then it was said among the nations,
   "The LORD has done great things for them."
The LORD has done great things for us,
   and we rejoiced. (Psalm 126:2–3)

Petitions

You have joined us together in one name and one sacred bond, and so we pray.
Response: We praise you, Lord.
You are Divine Parent and Author of Life; we are brothers and sisters to one another, and so we pray.
Our hearts are grateful for this reunion, and so we pray.
Add your own petitions.

Collect

Lord, from many places you have gathered people together to raise one voice in praise before you. Give us grateful hearts and memories born of your goodness.

Sharing of the Blessing Cup

Pray together the Our Father or sing a favorite family song.

For Vacation

Opening Prayer

We begin our journey to restore spirit and body in the name of the Father, and of the Son, and of the Holy Spirit.

Scripture

So when the crowd saw that neither Jesus nor his disciples were there, they themselves got into the boats and went to Capernaum looking for Jesus. When they found him on the other side of the sea, they said to him, "Rabbi, when did you come here?" (John 6:24–25)

Petitions

May we be safe as we renew ourselves through this time of rest, we pray.
Response: Be with us, Lord.
May we be recreated in your presence, we pray.
May we find joy and peace in our journey, we pray.
Add your own petitions.

Collect

Holier the people who labor, pray and play in your presence. In the sharing of this cup, may your love bind us together more closely.

Sharing of the Blessing Cup
Pray together the Our Father or sing a favorite song.

In Praise of Work

Opening Prayer

You blessed labor by the work of your own hands. We begin as Christians do everywhere in the name of the Father, and of the Son, and of the Holy Spirit.

Scripture

Do your best to present yourself to God as one approved by him, a worker who has no need to be ashamed, rightly explaining the word of truth. (2 Timothy 2:15)

Petitions

The dignity of labor is a blessing, we give thanks as your servants, we pray.
Response: We joyfully serve!
You help us provide for the needs of creation, we pray.
Make holy the work of our hands—may they be your hands, we pray.
Add your own petitions.

Collect

Unless you build a house, we who build it labor in vain.

Sharing of the Blessing Cup
Pray together the Our Father or sing an appropriate song.

PREPARING FOR THE FIRST DAY OF SCHOOL

Opening Prayer

This is a very special time: We celebrate _____'s first day of school, in the name of the Father, and of the Son, and of the Holy Spirit.

Scripture

Then [Jesus] went down with them and came to Nazareth, and was obedient to them. His mother treasured all these things in her heart.

And Jesus increased in wisdom and in years, and in divine and human favor. (Luke 2:51–52)

Petitions

Be with _____, we pray.

Response: May your angels protect him/her.

For _____'s teachers and new friends, we pray.

That the happiness that _____ brings to our home may be shared with all his/her school-mates, we pray.

That everyone in our family will listen and learn as Jesus did, we pray.

Add your own petitions.

Collect

Protect and keep each of us in your care. Help us to share the love our family has this day.

Sharing of the Blessing Cup

Pray together "Angel of God" or sing an appropriate song.

FOR THE BEGINNING OF THE SCHOOL YEAR

Opening Prayer

Lord, help us to progress steadily in wisdom, age and grace before you in the name of the Father, and of the Son, and of the Holy Spirit.

Scripture

I will instruct you and teach you the way you should go; I will counsel you with my eye upon you. (Psalm 32:8)

Petitions

Be with _____ and _____ as they begin another school year, we pray.
Response: Enlighten them, Lord.
May _____ build on the lessons already learned, we pray.
Let the spirit of our family be the gift that _____ shares with his/her teachers and school community.
Add your own petitions.

Collect

We know that you guide each of us. Give wisdom and understanding to _____, whom we send on his/her way this day.

Sharing of the Blessing Cup

Pray together the Our Father or sing an appropriate song.

For Graduation

Opening Prayer

On this occasion, we commemorate an important milestone. With joyful hearts we begin in the name of the Father, and of the Son, and of the Holy Spirit.

Scripture

Hold to the standard of sound teaching that you have heard in Christ Jesus. Guard the good treasure entrusted to you, with the help of the Holy Spirit living in us. (2 Timothy 1:13–14)

Petitions

For _____ and all those who graduate, we pray.
Response: We celebrate, Lord.
For teachers and their students, we pray.
With gratitude for this special occasion, we pray.
Add your own petitions.

Collect

We respect the trials and successes that have brought us to this point. Help us look upon this day with gratitude always, Lord, master teacher forever and ever.

Sharing of the Blessing Cup

Pray together the Our Father or sing an appropriate song.

CELEBRATING AN ACHIEVEMENT I

Opening Prayer

We humbly give thanks for the special strength you have given to us in _____. We celebrate in the name of the Father, and of the Son, and of the Holy Spirit.

Scripture

I have fought the good fight, I have finished the race, I have kept the faith. (2 Timothy 4:7)

Petitions

We pray for _____ on the occasion of _____, and we pray with joy.

Response: Glory to God!

We ask for the courage to accept our failures as well as our accomplishments, and we pray with joy.

We thank our God who is with us in good times and in bad, and we pray with joy.

Add your own petitions.

Collect

We thank you for loving us, God, so that we could be more than we could ever be alone. We glory in your goodness and praise you in all things.

Sharing of the Blessing Cup

Pray together the Our Father or sing an appropriate song.

CELEBRATING AN ACHIEVEMENT II

Opening Prayer

Joyfully we celebrate the success of _____ in _____, happily we celebrate in the name of the Father, and of the Son, and of the Holy Spirit.

Scripture

...they lean upon the LORD and say, "Surely the LORD is with us! No harm shall come upon us." (Micah 3:11)

Petitions

May _____ celebrate with joy this special achievement, we pray.
Response: Alleluia!
May we be found doing your will in all things, we pray.
With gratitude for your divine guidance, we pray.
Add your own petitions.

Collect

Joyfully in your presence we rejoice. Renew within us the energy to praise you above all.

Sharing of the Blessing Cup

Pray together the Our Father or sing an appropriate song.

AT A NEW BEGINNING

THIS SERVICE MAY ALSO BE USED TO BID FAREWELL TO MEMBERS LEAVING THE HOUSEHOLD FOR A LENGTHY PERIOD OF TIME.

Opening Prayer

With hope and fear in our hearts we celebrate a new beginning, in the name of the Father, and of the Son, and of the Holy Spirit.

Scripture

The LORD bless you and keep you;
the LORD make his face to shine upon you,
    and be gracious to you;
the LORD lift up his countenance upon you,
    and give you peace. (Numbers 6:24–26)

Petitions

Be with _____ as he/she moves in a new direction, Lord, we pray.
Response: You, Lord, are the beginning and the end.
May the sharing and caring of this family be with _____, Lord, we pray.
In the excitement of a new beginning, guide _____ and calm any anxiety or fears that may arise, Lord, we pray.
Add your own petitions.

Collect

We rejoice in a new beginning which _____ makes today. Guide and keep him/her in your care.

Sharing of the Blessing Cup
Pray together the Our Father or sing an appropriate song.

The Circle of Love

Happy is everyone who fears the
    LORD,
  who walks in his ways...
Your wife will be like a fruitful
    vine
  within your house;
Your children will be like olive
    shoots
  around your table.
Thus shall the man be blessed
  who fears the LORD.
(Psalm 128:1, 3–4)

Celebrating a Friendship

Opening Prayer

Our love for our friends is rooted in Christ Jesus, and so we begin in the name of the Father, and of the Son, and of the Holy Spirit.

Scripture

If in my name you ask me for anything, I will do it. If you love me, you will keep my commandments. And I will ask the Father, and he will give you another Advocate, to be with you forever. This is the Spirit of truth, whom the world cannot receive, because it neither sees him nor knows him. You know him, because he abides with you, and he will be in you. (John 14:14–17)

Petitions

Lord, we thank you for bringing _____ to share in this celebration. Hear us as we pray.
Response: Lord, be with us.
Lord, you made yourself known to a few, yet you are known by many because of your friends. Hear us as we pray.
Lord, give peace and happiness to _____. Hear us as we pray.
Add your own petitions.

Collect

Blessed are you, loving God, for all the works of your goodness. Most especially we thank you for one another in the sharing of this blessing cup. May it be a true sign of friendship.

Sharing of the Blessing Cup
Pray together the Our Father or sing an appropriate song.

For a Small Group I

Opening Prayer

Lord, help us to renew our faith in the name of the Father, and of the Son, and of the Holy Spirit.

Scripture

Again, truly I tell you, if two of you agree on earth about anything you ask, it will be done for you by my Father in heaven. For where two or three are gathered in my name, I am there among them. (Matthew 18:19–20)

Petitions

May our prayer rise like incense before you in the building up of the body of Christ, we pray.
Response: For you, O Christ.
As we study your word, may it burn deeply in our hearts, we pray.
In true evangelization, may we bring your message to each other and to the world, we pray.
Add your own petitions.

Collect

Lord, help us to make a friend, to be a friend and to bring a friend to Christ.

Sharing of the Blessing Cup

Pray or sing the Our Father or an appropriate song.

FOR A SMALL GROUP II

Opening Prayer

Help us to channel our lives in a ministry of service to others, in the name of the Father, and of the Son, and of the Holy Spirit.

Scripture

I am the vine, you are the branches. Those who abide in me and I in them bear much fruit, because apart from me you can do nothing.
(John 15:5)

Petitions

Draw us together in unity, we pray.
Response: We are your servants, Lord.
In allegiance and with a commitment to deep faith in God and the members of this community, we pray.
Show us how to serve one another as you care for us, we pray.
Add your own petitions.

Collect

We rejoice that you have chosen us to be bearers of good news.

Sharing of the Blessing Cup

Pray the Our Father or sing an appropriate song.

In Praise of Study Groups

Opening Prayer

We are drawn together to share the gift of knowledge in the name of the Father, and of the Son, and of the Holy Spirit.

Scripture

Are all apostles? Are all prophets? Are all teachers? Do all work miracles? Do all possess gifts of healing? Do all speak in tongues? Do all interpret? But strive for the greater gifts. And I will show you a still more excellent way.
(1 Corinthians 12:29–31)

Petitions

Bring us together, we pray.
Response: Make us one body.
May all study lead to the greatest gift—love, we pray.
May we discover you in our support for one another, we pray.
Add your own petitions.

Collect

Teach us patience and kindness. Teach us to rejoice in what is right. Help us to trust and hope. Remove from us any obstacle to your goodness. Then we shall rest in your love.

Sharing of the Blessing Cup
Pray together the Our Father or sing an appropriate song.

THANKSGIVING FOR VOLUNTEERS

Opening Prayer

We happily gather to celebrate being coworkers among God's people in the name of the Father, and of the Son, and of the Holy Spirit.

Scripture

Then I heard the voice of the Lord saying, "Whom shall I send, and who will go for us?" And I said, "Here am I; send me!" (Isaiah 6:8)

Petitions

Guide us as we learn from the people we are sent to serve in your name, we pray.
Response: Bless us, Lord.
Whenever we gather, we trust you are present among us, we pray.
May _____ be a reflection of your gentle care, we pray.
Add your own petitions.

Collect

We rejoice in sending forth _____. Be their safety and guide.

Sharing of the Blessing Cup

Extend hand over the one(s) being sent and pray or sing a blessing.

FOR A LOCAL FAITH COMMUNITY

Opening Prayer

Brought together in faith and united in a common mission, we commit ourselves to each other in the name of the Father, and of the Son, and of the Holy Spirit.

Scripture

But speaking the truth in love, we must grow up in every way into him who is the head, into Christ, from whom the whole body, joined and knit together by every ligament with which it is equipped, as each part is working properly, promotes the body's growth in building itself up in love. (Ephesians 4:15–16)

Petitions

For the members of _____ parish family, we pray.
Response: Bind us together.
For strength to remain faithful to the teachings of the gospel, our patrons and the church, we pray.
For courage to hold fast as a community of believers embarked on a journey of faith, we pray.
Add your own petitions.

Collect

With one mind and heart, one God of us all, we proclaim one faith through Christ Jesus our Lord.

Sharing of the Blessing Cup
Pray the Our Father or sing "One Bread, One Body," or another appropriate song.

In Praise of Nature

Opening Prayer

All seasons give praise to the Creator, and so we pray in the name of the Father, and of the Son, and of the Holy Spirit.

Scripture

Blessed by the LORD be his land,
　　with the choice gifts of heaven above,
　　and of the deep that lies beneath;
with the choice fruits of the sun,
　　and the rich yield of the months;
with the finest produce of the
　　　　ancient mountains,
　　and the abundance of the
　　　　everlasting hills;
with the choice gifts of the earth
　　　　and its fullness....
(Deuteronomy 33:13b–16a)

Petitions

We praise you, Lord, as master of all seasons and times, and we say…
Response: Blessed be God!
We give you thanks for the gift of life, and we say…
In all that you have created we see your glory, and we say...
Add your own petitions.

Collect

Creator God, we thank you for Jesus, your Son, who lights the darkness of our hearts. Send your Spirit and renew your creation.

Sharing of the Blessing Cup

Pray together the Our Father or sing an appropriate song.

WITH RESPECT FOR THE EARTH

Opening Prayer

The delicate balance of your created goodness
has been entrusted to us as caretakers. And so we
begin in the name of the Father, and of the Son,
and of the Holy Spirit.

Scripture

How desirable are all his works,
and how sparkling they are to see!
All these things live and remain forever;
each creature is preserved to meet a
particular need.
All things come in pairs, one opposite the other,
and he has made nothing incomplete.
Each supplements the virtues of the other.
Who could ever tire of seeing his glory?
(Sirach 42:22–25)

Petitions

For the integrity of creation, we pray.
Response: Lord, govern us with justice and peace.
For a deeper awareness of our limited resources
and your boundless mercy, we pray.
For guidance in using wisely the things of this
earth, we pray.
Add your own petitions.

Collect

The earth is full of the goodness of the Lord. Let
us be glad and rejoice.

Sharing of the Blessing Cup

*Pray together the Our Father, or sing the Prayer of
Saint Francis or some other appropriate hymn or
song.*

FOR GARDENERS AND THE HARVEST

Opening Prayer

Reflecting on the bounty and the variety of nourishment that comes from the earth, we pray in the name of the Father, and of the Son, and of the Holy Spirit.

Scripture

The kingdom of God is as if someone would scatter seed on the ground.... The earth produces of itself, first the stalk, then the head, then the full grain in the head. But when the grain is ripe, at once he goes in with his sickle, because the harvest has come. (Mark 4:26–29)

Petitions

Through the work of our hands, we pray.
Response: Bless us, Lord.
With gentle rains and fertile soil, we pray.
For those who are hungry, we pray.
Add your own petitions.

Collect

The wonders of a productive land yield a hundredfold.

Sharing of the Blessing Cup
Pray the Our Father or sing an appropriate song.

In Times of Need

...for I know that through your prayers and the help of the Spirit of Jesus Christ this will turn out for my deliverance. It is my eager expectation and hope that I will not be put to shame in any way, but that by my speaking with all boldness, Christ will be exalted...

(Philippians 1:19–20)

In Time of Natural Disaster

Opening Prayer

At a time when emptiness and sorrow surround us, we turn to God for hope and consolation. We pray in the name of the Father, and of the Son, and of the Holy Spirit.

Scripture

I waited patiently for the LORD; he inclined to me and heard my cry. He drew me up from the desolate pit, out of the miry bog, and set my feet upon a rock, making my steps secure. He put a new song in my mouth, a song of praise to our God. Many will see and fear, and put their trust in the LORD. Happy are those who make the LORD their trust....(Psalm 40:1–4a)

Petitions

We have seen, Lord, your mighty power over earth and heavens and we pray.
Response: God of might, protect us.
In your goodness, Lord, you have been our shelter, we pray.
Give your courage to those who are sad and broken, we pray.
Add your own petitions.

Collect

Mindful of your dominion over all things, we offer this prayer. We ask your guidance and protection. Lead us to do your will with careful concern for all that has been entrusted to us.

Sharing of the Blessing Cup
Pray together the Our Father or sing an appropriate song, such as "Amazing Grace."

In Time of Misfortune or Hardship

Opening Prayer

You know us, Lord, so we turn to you at this time of testing, praying in the name of the Father, and of the Son, and of the Holy Spirit.

Scripture

So we do not lose heart. Even though our outer nature is wasting away, our inner nature is being renewed day by day. For this slight momentary affliction is preparing us for an eternal weight of glory beyond all measure, because we look not at what can be seen but at what cannot be seen; for what can be seen is temporary, but what cannot be seen is eternal. (2 Corinthians 4:16–18)

Petitions

We ask you to help us in this time of need, especially _____, we pray.

Response: Be with us, Lord.

Help us to walk by faith, knowing that you will bring good out of every difficulty, we pray.

We thank you for the many gifts you have given to us through this difficult time, and we pray.

Add your own petitions.

Collect

Lord Jesus, as you lived on this earth you showed us how to deal with trials and hardships. Be with us now. Teach us how to trust in you.

Sharing of the Blessing Cup

Pray together the Our Father or sing an appropriate song, such as "He's Got the Whole World in His Hands."

In Time of Trouble

Opening Prayer

Jesus said, "Do not let your hearts be troubled. Have faith in God and faith in me...." And so we begin in the name of the Father, and of the Son, and of the Holy Spirit.

Scripture

...If God is for us, who is against us? He who did not withhold his own Son, but gave him up for all of us, will he not with him also give us everything else? (Romans 8:31–32)

Petitions

Show us your mercy and love, we pray.
Response: We trust you, Lord.
Help us in these difficult times, we pray.
Stay with us in these troubled times, we pray.
Add your own petitions.

Collect

Our hearts are restless, O Lord, until they rest in you.

Sharing of the Blessing Cup

Pray together the Our Father or sing an appropriate song, such as "Be With Us, Lord."

AT THE COMPLETION OF AN EVENT OR TIME OF LIFE

Opening Prayer

We give thanks for your guidance and goodness in the name of the Father, and of the Son, and of the Holy Spirit.

Scripture

...with fear and great joy, [they] ran to tell his disciples. Suddenly Jesus met them and said, "Greetings!" (Matthew 28:8–9)

Petitions

Thank you for walking with us at this time of our life, we pray.
Response: We are grateful, O Lord.
Help us to look with anticipation to the new adventures that you promised us, we pray.
Together may we walk with you in life's journey, we pray.
Add your own petitions.

Collect

With gratitude we have trusted in your guidance and have not been disappointed. Help us to begin again to do good in your name.

Sharing of the Blessing Cup
Pray together the Our Father or sing an appropriate song.

WHEN SOMEONE IS ILL

Opening Prayer

In faith we pray for _____, who shares in the suffering of Christ, in the name of the Father, and of the Son, and of the Holy Spirit.

Scripture

Are any among you suffering? They should pray. Are any cheerful? They should sing songs of praise. Are any among you sick? They should call for the elders of the church and have them pray over them, anointing them with oil in the name of the Lord. The prayer of faith will save the sick, and the Lord will raise them up.... (James 5:13–15a)

Petitions

Bless _____, who is in need of your healing power, we pray, Lord.
Response: Thy will be done.
For doctors, nurses and technicians who share in the healing ministry of Christ, we pray, Lord.
For all the sick and suffering, we pray, Lord.
Add your own petitions.

Collect

O God, send your healing power upon those for whom we pray. We ask this through Jesus Christ, your Son, our Lord.

Sharing of the Blessing Cup
Pray together the Our Father or sing an appropriate song.

FOR THOSE WHO CARE FOR THE SICK

For home visitors, hospice workers, eucharistic ministers, etc.

Opening Prayer

We join together in mutual prayer and encouragement for those who minister to our loved ones who are sick. We begin in the name of the Father, and of the Son, and of the Holy Spirit.

Scripture

Beloved, you do faithfully whatever you do for the friends, even though they are strangers to you; they have testified to your love before the church. You will do well to send them on in the manner worthy of God; for they began their journey for the sake of Christ.... (3 John 5–7a)

Petitions

On this day we welcome _____ as a minister to the sick, and we pray.
Response: Divine Healer, be with us.
Guide your people in service and ministry to the infirm, we pray.
Help us to see the suffering Christ in all who are afflicted, we pray.
Add your own petitions.

Collect

Join us together in steadfast service and gentle support for your people. We pray in the name of Jesus, our Lord.

Sharing of the Blessing Cup
Pray together the Our Father or sing an appropriate song, such as "Lay Your Hands."

FOR SPECIAL NEEDS

Opening Prayer
> You ask us to come to you with our burdens and so we begin with the name of the Father, and of the Son, and of the Holy Spirit.

Scripture
> Ask, and it will be given you; search, and you will find; knock, and the door will be opened for you. (Matthew 7:7)

Petitions
> Hearts filled with trust, we come to you with very special needs, we pray.
> *Response:* Grant us your wisdom, Lord.
> Send us your wisdom. Hear the prayer we offer in faith, we pray.
> Open for us avenues of understanding, we pray.
> *Add your own petitions.*

Collect
> As we ask, seek and knock, we are confident that we shall receive, it shall be opened and your will made clear.

Sharing of the Blessing Cup
> *Pray the Our Father or sing an appropriate song.*

ON THE DEATH OF A LOVED ONE

Opening Prayer

Our hearts are heavy as we pray in the name of the Father, and of the Son, and of the Holy Spirit.

Scripture

Martha said to Jesus, "Lord, if you had been here, my brother would not have died. But even now I know that God will give you whatever you ask of him." Jesus said to her, "Your brother will rise again." Martha said to him, "I know that he will rise again in the resurrection on the last day." Jesus said to her, "I am the resurrection and the life. Those who believe in me, even though they die, will live, and everyone who lives and believes in me will never die. Do you believe this?" She said to him, "Yes, Lord. I believe that you are the Messiah, the Son of God, the one coming into the world." (John 11:21–27)

Petitions

We thank you for the life of _____, whom you love and whom we love.
Response: You are the resurrection and the life.
We pray for healing of all the unhappy feelings _____'s death leaves in our hearts.
We pray that _____ will share in the glory of your love for all eternity.
Add your own petitions.

Collect

Be with us, Lord. We trust in you and hope in your glorious Resurrection. We lift up the cup of sorrow, confident that you will change our mourning to rejoicing.

Sharing of the Blessing Cup
  *Pray together the Our Father or sing an appropriate
  song, such as "I Am the Bread of Life."*

On the Death of a Pet

Opening Prayer

Master and Lord of all creation, hear the prayer
we offer you in the name of the Father, and of the
Son, and of the Holy Spirit.

Scripture

Are not five sparrows sold for two pennies? Yet
not one of them is forgotten in God's sight. (Luke
12:6)

Petitions

You have shown us affection and faithfulness
through all of creation. We are grateful as we pray.
Response: Comfort us, Lord.
We remember the laughter and joy that _____
has given us, and we pray.
Help us to share kindness and care with all living
things, we pray.
Add your own petitions.

Collect

In your goodness you have called us to be stewards of all creation. We take up this cup, grateful
for having been entrusted with the care of this
creature. We marvel at how you have fashioned
and formed our world in harmony and peace.

Sharing of the Blessing Cup
Pray together the Our Father.

FOR PEACE

Opening Prayer

May our hearts be restless until they rest in you in the name of the Father, and of the Son, and of the Holy Spirit.

Scripture

And we urge you, beloved to admonish the idlers, encourage the faint hearted, help the weak, be patient with all of them. See that none of you repays evil for evil, but always seek to do good to one another and to all. (1 Thessalonians 5:14–15)

Petitions

Help us to work for justice in our world, we pray.
Response: Grant us peace.
For the integrity of creation, we pray.
Place your Spirit in our hearts and homes, we pray.
Add your own petitions.

Collect

May the God of peace make us perfect in holiness...spirit, soul, and body, so that we may be a source of peace for others.

Sharing of the Blessing Cup

Pray together the Our Father or sing "Let There Be Peace on Earth" or another appropriate song.

Milestones of Christian Life

Know that the LORD is God.
It is he that made us, and we
are his;
we are his people, and the
sheep of his pasture.

Enter his gates with thanksgiving,
and his courts with praise;
Give thanks to him, bless his
name.

For the LORD is good;
his steadfast love endures forever,
and his faithfulness to all
generations.
(Psalm 100:3–5)

CELEBRATION OF A BAPTISM

Opening Prayer

We celebrate the rebirth of _____ in the waters of baptism in the name of the Father, and of the Son, and of the Holy Spirit.

Scripture

People were bringing little children to him in order that he might touch them; and the disciples spoke sternly to them. But when Jesus saw this, he was indignant and said to them, "Let the little children come to me; do not stop them; for it is to such as these that the kingdom of God belongs. Truly I tell you, whoever does not receive the kingdom of God as a little child will never enter it." And he took them up in his arms, laid his hands on them, and blessed them.
(Mark 10:13–16)

Petitions

By the waters of baptism, bathe _____ in your love, we pray.
Response: Wash us clean, O Lord.
By our celebration of this event, renew within us the saving power of our baptism, we pray.
As members of your family, may we together give praise to God, we pray.
Add your own petitions.

Collect

You have made us one by the saving mystery of baptism. Help us now to be refreshed at the living spring of your goodness in each person.

Sharing of the Blessing Cup
Pray together the Our Father or sing an appropriate song.

For a Name Day

Opening Prayer

Lord, on this day we pause to remember those for whom we are named. In that spirit, we begin in the name of the Father, and of the Son, and of the Holy Spirit.

Scripture

You are the light of the world. A city built on a hill cannot be hid. No one after lighting a lamp puts it under the bushel basket, but on the lampstand, and it gives light to all in the house. In the same way, let your light shine before others, so that they may see your good works and give glory to your Father in heaven. (Matthew 5:14–16)

Someone may wish to tell the story of the saint who is being commemorated or something about the person for whom the one being honored is named.

Petitions

Lord God, keep us ever faithful to the spirit and example of those for whom we are named, we pray.
Response: Lord, hear our prayer.
Help us to live holy lives in the image of _____, we pray.
May we be counted among your saints, we pray.
Add your own petitions.

Collect

Lord Jesus, direct us in the way you would have us go so that we may share the life of the saints forever.

Sharing of the Blessing Cup

Pray together the Our Father, or sing "For All the Saints" or "When the Saints Go Marching In."

In Honor of First Reconciliation

Opening Prayer

We celebrate your forgiveness in our family in the name of the Father, and of the Son, and of the Holy Spirit.

Scripture

Jesus said to them again, "Peace be with you. As the Father has sent me, so I send you." When he had said this, he breathed on them and said to them, "Receive the Holy Spirit. If you forgive the sins of any, they are forgiven them; if you retain the sins of any, they are retained." (John 20:21–23)

Petitions

For _____, who celebrates forgiveness this day, we pray.

Response: My Lord and my God.

That we readily forgive one another as Christ forgives us, we pray.

That we celebrate the healing power of Jesus in our lives, we pray.

Add your own petitions.

Collect

We lift up to you a cup of healing and celebration. May we overflow with the joy of forgiveness.

Sharing of the Blessing Cup

Pray an act of contrition or sing "Now Thank We All Our God."

In Honor of a First Communion

Opening Prayer

Today we celebrate the wonderful promise of the Last Supper, in the name of the Father, and of the Son, and of the Holy Spirit.

Scripture

While they were eating, Jesus took a loaf of bread, and after blessing it he broke it, gave it to the disciples, and said, "Take, eat; this is my body." Then he took a cup, and after giving thanks he gave it to them, saying, "Drink from it, all of you; for this is my blood of the covenant, which is poured out for many for the forgiveness of sins." (Matthew 26:26–28)

Petitions

We are grateful for the bread of life you give us. With joy, we pray.

Response: Lord Jesus, you are the bread of life.

We thank you and praise you for _____'s First Communion, which we celebrate. With joy, we pray.

May we all be one at your eternal banquet forever. With joy, we pray.

Add your own petitions.

Collect

Lord, we thank you for the wonderful gift of your unconditional love for us. May we grow closer to you and to each other in the sacrament of the Eucharist.

Sharing of the Blessing Cup

Pray together the Our Father or sing an appropriate song.

IN PREPARATION FOR CONFIRMATION

Opening Prayer

With the hopeful promise of your guidance, we pray in the name of the Father, and of the Son, and of the Holy Spirit.

Scripture

When the day of Pentecost had come, they were all together in one place. And suddenly from heaven there came a sound like the rush of a violent wind, and it filled the entire house where they were sitting. Divided tongues, as of fire, appeared among them, and a tongue rested on each of them. All of them were filled with the Holy Spirit and began to speak in other languages, as the Spirit gave them ability. (Acts 2:1–4)

Petitions

We pray that _____ will be filled with the grace and power of your Spirit. Hear our prayer, Lord.

Response: Send your Spirit, Lord.

We pray that all of us will be living examples of Christ's life for each other. Hear our prayer, Lord.

We pray that _____ may joyfully serve the church. Hear our prayer, Lord.

Add your own petitions.

Collect

Lord, complete the calling you gave us at baptism and Eucharist. In the power of your Spirit, let us proclaim your goodness to the ends of the earth.

Sharing of the Blessing Cup

Pray together the Our Father or sing an appropriate song, such as "Come, Holy Ghost."

On Being a Sponsor

Opening Prayer

_____ has been selected as an example of living faith in the name of the Father, and of the Son, and of the Holy Spirit.

Scripture

I, John, your brother...was on the island called Patmos because of the word of God and the testimony of Jesus. I was in the spirit on the Lord's day, and I heard behind me a loud voice like a trumpet saying, "Write in a book what you see...." (Revelation 1:9–11)

Petitions

For _____ and his/her sponsor _____, who this day look toward a spiritual relationship in Christ Jesus, we pray.

Response: Be with them, Lord.

In preparation for this sacrament may _____ and _____ be enlightened by the Holy Spirit, we pray.

May _____ and _____ witness Christ to one another, we pray.

Add your own petitions.

Collect

Bring us to a deeper awareness of our responsibility as witnesses of Christ Jesus our Lord.

Sharing of the Blessing Cup

Pray together the Our Father or sing "Sing a New Song unto the Lord."

For Profession of Faith

Opening Prayer

As we begin a journey of faith, may we walk with each other in the name of the Father, and of the Son, and of the Holy Spirit.

Scripture

Come to me, all you that are weary and are carrying heavy burdens, and I will give you rest. Take my yoke upon you, and learn from me; for I am gentle and humble in heart, and you will find rest for your souls. For my yoke is easy, and my burden light. (Matthew 11:28–30)

Litany

Do you reject Satan?

Response: I do.

And all his works?

And all his empty promises?

Do you believe in God, the Father Almighty, Creator of Heaven and Earth?

Do you believe in Jesus Christ, God's only son, our Lord who was born of the Virgin Mary, was crucified, died and was buried, rose from the dead, and is now seated at the right hand of the Father?

Do you believe in the Holy Spirit, the Holy Catholic church, the communion of saints, the forgiveness of sins, the resurrection of the body, and life everlasting?

Collect

Place within our hearts a desire for you above all else and strengthen our resolve to seek you in word and sacrament.

Sharing of the Blessing Cup

Sing an appropriate song, such as "Earthen Vessels" or "Be Not Afraid."

Announcing an Engagement

Opening Prayer

From the beginning of time you reminded us that it is not good to be alone. With reverence and joy we celebrate a promise to marry, in the name of the Father, and of the Son, and of the Holy Spirit.

Scripture

Therefore a man leaves his father and his mother and clings to his wife, and they become one flesh. (Genesis 2:24)

Those intending marriage then read this pledge:

And I will take you for my wife (husband) forever; I will take you for my wife (husband) in righteousness and in justice, in steadfast love, and in mercy. I will take you for my wife (husband) in faithfulness; and you shall know the Lord (based on Hosea 2:19–20).

Petitions

Trusting in your divine guidance, we pray.
Response: Bring us closer to you and to each other.
Unite _____ and _____ in a joyful new beginning, we pray.
Thank you for leading us to this wonderful celebration of your love for us, we pray.
Unite our families in your love, we pray.
Add your own petitions.

Collect

In the midst of our celebration and preparations, may our first thought be for enriching the special grace and love entrusted to _____ and _____ this day.

Sharing of the Blessing Cup
Pray together the Our Father or sing an appropriate song.

In Honor of a Marriage

THIS SERVICE MAY BE USED TO CELEBRATE A WEDDING OR AN ANNIVERSARY.

Opening Prayer

God of love, we commemorate with joy your presence in our life. In that spirit we celebrate the gift of your sacrament of marriage, in the name of the Father, and of the Son, and of the Holy Spirit.

Scripture

Do not press me to leave you
　or to turn back from following you!
Where you go, I will go;
　Where you lodge, I will lodge;
your people shall be my people,
　and your God my God.
Where you die, I will die—
　there I will be buried. (Ruth 1:16–17a)

Petitions

Lord, you blessed the marriage feast at Cana; now bless _____ and _____, we pray.
Response: Keep us in your love, Lord.
Let the love they have for each other be a faithful reflection of your love, we pray.
Bless all called to share in this sacrament with an abundance of your goodness, we pray.
Add your own petitions.

Collect

We raise the cup of blessing to celebrate the promise of love man and woman make before God. May the covenant of love we celebrate today bring us to eternal life in your love.

Sharing of the Blessing Cup
Pray together the Our Father or sing an appropriate song.

For a Wedding Anniversary

Opening Prayer

Your gift of married love is our celebration this day in the name of the Father, and of the Son, and of the Holy Spirit.

Scripture

"For this reason a man shall leave his father and mother and be joined to his wife, and the two shall become one flesh." So they are no longer two, but one flesh. Therefore what God has joined together, let no one separate. (Mark 10:7–9)

Petitions

May the grace of this sacrament of matrimony be cause for rejoicing this day, we pray.
Response: Renew your love within them.
May _____ and _____ know your love always, we pray.
Help them to be a model of Christian marriage for others, we pray.
Add your own petitions.

Collect

We praise you for the vows this couple made in your presence. Strengthen them daily with the guidance of your Spirit.

Sharing of the Blessing Cup
Pray together the Our Father or sing an appropriate song.

ON THE OCCASION OR JUBILEE OF RELIGIOUS VOWS OR ORDINATION

Opening Prayer

We praise and thank you in your servant _____ for the wonderful gifts you bestow on your people, in the name of the Father, and of the Son, and of the Holy Spirit.

Scripture

What shall I return to the LORD
   for all his bounty to me?
I will lift up the cup of salvation
   and call on the name of the LORD,
I will pay my vows to the LORD
   in the presence of all his people.
Precious in the sight of the LORD
   is the death of his faithful ones.
O LORD, I am your servant,
   I am your servant, the child of your serving girl.
   You have loosed my bonds.
I will offer to you a thanksgiving sacrifice
   and call on the name of the LORD.
I will pay my vows to the LORD
   in the presence of all his people...
(Psalm 116:12–18)

Petitions

God in heaven, we ask your blessing on _____, your servant, as we pray.
Response: Lord, be with your servant.
We rejoice in the gift of Spirit which fills _____, as we pray.
May your people be willing to hear the good news proclaimed by _____, we pray.
Add your own petitions.

Collect

A joyful cup of celebration we raise in honor of
_____. You, Lord, are the eternal shepherd
who inspires those who lead the Christian community. We give praise and rejoice.

Sharing of the Blessing Cup
Pray together the Our Father or sing an appropriate
song.

FOR VOCATIONS TO MINISTRY IN THE CHURCH

Opening Prayer

In every age leaders are called from the community to proclaim the message of Jesus. For the needs of our own age we pray in the name of the Father, and of the Son, and of the Holy Spirit.

Scripture

As you go, proclaim the good news, "The kingdom of heaven has come near." Cure the sick, raise the dead, cleanse the lepers, cast out demons. You received without payment; give without payment. (Matthew 10:7–8)

Petitions

That priests, brothers, sisters and deacons will grow in the spirit of Christ Jesus, we pray.
Response: Send laborers into the harvest, Lord.
For those who serve our parish in lay ministries, we pray.
That men and women everywhere will hear God's call to them and find the grace and the courage to answer, we pray.
Lord, help us to learn by listening so that we may carry out the mission of evangelization, we pray.
Add your own petitions.

Collect

Lord, we recommit ourselves to serving the church with hope and enthusiasm. Help us to recognize the needs of our faith community and to serve it better.

Sharing of the Blessing Cup
Pray together the Our Father or sing an appropriate song, such as "Here I Am, Lord."

Holy Days and Holidays

The pastures of the wilderness overflow,
   the hills gird themselves with joy,
the meadows clothe themselves with flocks,
   the valleys deck themselves with grain,
   they shout and sing together for joy.
   (Psalm 65:12–13)

The Beginning of a New Year I

Opening Prayer

Today we begin again to set our priorities and direction, in the name of the Father, and of the Son, and of the Holy Spirit.

Scripture

For everything there is a season, and a time for every matter under heaven:

a time to be born, and a time to die;

a time to plant, and a time to pluck up what is planted;

a time to kill, and a time to heal;

a time to break down, and a time to build up;

a time to weep, and a time to laugh;

a time to mourn, and a time to dance;

a time to throw away stones, and a time to gather stones together;

a time to embrace, and a time to refrain from embracing;

a time to seek, and a time to lose;

a time to keep, and a time to throw away;

a time to tear, and a time to sew;

a time to keep silence, and a time to speak;

a time to love, and a time to hate;

a time for war, and a time for peace.

(Ecclesiastes 3:1–8)

Petitions:

At the beginning of this new year, we leave what is past and look toward that which is in store for us in Christ Jesus, as we pray.

Response: Lead us, Lord.

Keep us focused on each new day that you grant to us, Lord, we pray.

Strengthen our resolve to do your will in all things,
we pray.
Add your own petitions.

Collect

May this be a year of grace. May we be a daily
sign of your presence. May all things work together for the good in Christ Jesus.

Sharing of the Blessing Cup

*Pray together the Our Father or sing an appropriate
song.*

THE BEGINNING OF A NEW YEAR II

Opening Prayer

As the old year fades and the new is on the horizon, we begin in the name of the Father, and of the Son, and of the Holy Spirit.

Scripture

The spirit of the Lord GOD is upon me,
because the LORD has anointed me;
he has sent me to bring good news to the
oppressed,
to bind up the brokenhearted,
to proclaim liberty to the captives,
and release to the prisoners;
to proclaim the year of the LORD'S favor,
and the day of vengeance of our God;
to comfort all who mourn....
(Isaiah 61:1–2)

Petitions

Help us to begin anew in the Lord who gives dawn to each day, we pray.
Response: Be with us, Lord.
May our hope and trust be in you, we pray.
Make us ready to do your will, we pray.
Add your own petitions

Collect

By your grace, may we live as beacons of your glory in all you ask us to do.

Sharing of the Blessing Cup

Pray together the Our Father or sing an appropriate song.

On Epiphany

Opening Prayer

Following the light of the Christmas star, we give praise through Gaspar, Melchior and Balthasar and pray in the name of the Father, and of the Son, and of the Holy Spirit.

Scripture

When they saw that the star had stopped, they were overwhelmed with joy. On entering the house, they saw the child with Mary his mother; and they knelt down and paid him homage. Then, opening their treasure chests, they offered him gifts of gold, frankincense, and myrrh. (Matthew 2:10–11)

Petitions

Lord, as you have gifted us may we in turn gift others with your presence, we pray.
Response: Draw us to the light, Lord.
Guide us as we search for you, we pray.
Help us to celebrate always Christ among us, we pray.
Add your own petitions.

Collect

Make straight our way and clear the path that leads to you.

Sharing of the Blessing Cup
Pray together the Our Father or sing an appropriate song such as "We Three Kings."

On Valentine's Day

Opening Prayer

Recalling God's love, we begin in the name of the Father, and of the Son, and of the Holy Spirit.

Scripture

Beloved, since God loved us so much, we also ought to love one another.... There is no fear in love, but perfect love casts out fear.... We love because he first loved us. (1 John 4:11–19)

Petitions

May we walk in the presence of you who first loved us, we pray.
Response: Keep us in your love.
For those who complete our spirit, we pray.
By every act of kindness, we pray.
Add your own petitions.

Collect

Through the legend of Saint Valentine, we are reminded of our need to be loved and to love. Like Valentine, teach others the way that leads to you.

Sharing of the Blessing Cup

Pray together the Our Father or sing an appropriate song.

LENTEN SERVICE I

Opening Prayer

Lent reminds us to pray and to do penance, and so we begin in the name of the Father, and of the Son, and of the Holy Spirit.

Scripture

Then Jesus was led up by the Spirit into the wilderness to be tempted by the devil. He fasted forty days and forty nights, and afterwards he was famished. (Matthew 4:1–2)

Petitions

Change our hearts and renew our love for you, Lord, we pray.
Response: Be with us, Lord.
Help us to bring order into our lives so that others may find you there, Lord, we pray.
By sharing your suffering may we also come to rejoice in your Resurrection, Lord, we pray.
Add your own petitions.

Collect

Lord, be with us as we look forward to new birth at Easter. Let us shine forth with the joy of your rising.

Sharing of the Blessing Cup
Pray together the Our Father or sing an appropriate Lenten song.

LENTEN SERVICE II

Opening Prayer

As we journey toward the feast of the Resurrection, be with us in the name of the Father, and of the Son, and of the Holy Spirit.

Scripture

... Jesus took with him Peter and James and his brother John and led them up a high mountain, by themselves. And he was transfigured before them, and his face shone like the sun, and his clothes became dazzling white. (Matthew 17:1–2)

Petitions

Transform us into living witnesses of your gospel, we pray.

Response: Change our hearts, Lord.

Guide us through our prayer, fasting and almsgiving to a deeper awareness of you in each other, we pray.

Add your own petitions.

Collect

For us, Lord, this time is one of pruning so that we can bear the fruit of your goodness in our every thought, word and action.

Sharing of the Blessing Cup

Pray together the Our Father or sing an appropriate Lenten song.

Lenten Service III

Opening Prayer

We prepare our hearts for the joy of the Resurrection in the name of the Father, and of the Son, and of the Holy Spirit.

Scripture

Rejoice in the Lord always; again I will say, Rejoice. Let your gentleness be known to everyone. The Lord is near. Do not worry about anything, but in everything by prayer and supplication with thanksgiving let your requests be made known to God. And the peace of God, which surpasses all understanding, will guard your hearts and your minds in Christ Jesus.
(Philippians 4:4–7)

Petitions

Through our boldness of prayer may we grow in gentleness of spirit, we pray.
Response: Make us new.
By fasting help us to hunger for your love, we pray.
In almsgiving may we touch the most needy of your people, we pray.
Add your own petitions.

Collect

Through our Lenten practices lead us to a deeper awareness of you, our crucified and risen Savior.

Sharing of the Blessing Cup
Pray together the Our Father or sing an appropriate Lenten song.

A HOLY WEEK GATHERING

Opening Prayer

As we approach the most sacred of all Christian feasts, we ask guidance in the name of the Father, and of the Son, and of the Holy Spirit.

Scripture

...God anointed Jesus of Nazareth with the Holy Spirit and with power; ...he went about doing good and healing all who were oppressed by the devil, for God was with him. We are witnesses to all that he did both in Judea and in Jerusalem. They put him to death by hanging him on a tree...
(Acts 10:38–39)

Petitions

As we draw near to the end of our Lenten journey we pray.
Response: Lead us, Lord.
May we break bread and share the cup, ever mindful of your presence among us, we pray.
With hope in your life, death and resurrection we join together and pray.
May this cup of blessing that reflects both sorrow and joy bind us together as your people, we pray.
Add your own petitions.

Collect

This Holy Week leads us to Christ, our hope and salvation. Bring us from darkness to light.

Sharing of the Blessing Cup

Pray together the Our Father or sing an appropriate Lenten song.

EASTER CELEBRATION

Opening Prayer

The Lord is risen, alleluia! Let us celebrate in the name of the Father, and of the Son, and of the Holy Spirit.

Scripture

...[W]hen [the women] went [into the tomb], they did not find the body. While they were perplexed about this, suddenly two men in dazzling clothes stood beside them. The women were terrified and bowed their faces to the ground, but the men said to them, "Why do you look for the living among the dead? He is not here, but has risen. Remember how he told you, while he was still in Galilee, that the Son of Man must be handed over to sinners, and be crucified, and on the third day rise again." Then they remembered his words... (Luke 24:3–8)

Petitions

In his rising from the dead, Jesus has given us the power to rise above ourselves; may we walk in the light that brightens the path of faith, we pray.
Response: Alleluia!
May the Lord be with us as he was with the faithful on that first Easter, we pray.
May this cup be a sign of joy—the joy of Christians renewed by Christ's rising, we pray.
Add your own petitions.

Collect

Help us, Lord, to rise above ourselves. Break our hearts of stone so that we truly may shine as children of light and life.

Sharing of the Blessing Cup
Pray together the Our Father or sing an appropriate Easter song or an alleluia.

On Ascension

Opening Prayer

We stand in awe as earth is united to heaven in the name of the Father, and of the Son, and of the Holy Spirit.

Scripture

I am ascending to my Father and your Father, to my God and your God! (John 20:17)

Petitions

Looking toward the heavens, we pray to be united one day with our heavenly Father, the saints and our family.

Response: Glory and praise to you, Lord.

In faith we look toward Christ coming among us again.

We long for the unity of all God's creation.

Add your own petitions.

Collect

Restless is the heart that seeks you. May we find peace without end.

Sharing of the Blessing Cup

Pray together the Our Father or sing an appropriate alleluia song.

MOTHER'S OR FATHER'S DAY

Opening Prayer

Our first teachers are our parents. We pray for them in a special way this day, in the name of the Father, and of the Son, and of the Holy Spirit.

Scripture

For this reason I bow my knees before the Father, from whom every family in heaven and on earth takes its name. I pray that, according to the riches of his glory, he may grant that you may be strengthened in your inner being with power through his Spirit... (Ephesians 3:14–16)

Petitions

Grant your blessing to our mother/father on this special day which honors her/him.
Response: Bless our mother/father, Lord.
Keep us in your care so that we may live in the pattern of the Holy Family, we pray.
For those who have not been blessed with the love that fills our home, we pray.
Add your own petitions.

Collect

Lord, we thank you for allowing us to celebrate this special day. May we continue to live the lessons we have learned from our parents.

Sharing of the Blessing Cup
Pray together the Our Father or Hail Mary, or sing an appropriate song.

FOR CIVIC HOLIDAYS

Opening Prayer
In peace we place ourselves before you, celebrating the freedom which you have granted to us, in the name of the Father, and of the Son, and of the Holy Spirit.

Scripture
...[Y]ou shall proclaim liberty throughout the land to all its inhabitants. It shall be a jubilee for you... (Leviticus 25:10b)

Petitions
Continue to pour out your kindness on the people you have called by name, we pray.
Response: Grant us your freedom, Lord.
Hold us secure in the hollow of your hand, we pray.
Keep us ever mindful of the great grace you have entrusted to us, our liberty, we pray.
Add your own petitions.

Collect
Send us your Spirit, Lord, and make us proclaimers of the Good News so that all may celebrate your freedom and blessing.

Sharing of the Blessing Cup
Pray together the Our Father or sing an appropriate national song.

ON THE FEAST OF SAINT FRANCIS OF ASSISI (OCTOBER 4)

Opening Prayer

In simple joy we pray in the name of the Father, and of the Son, and of the Holy Spirit.

Scripture

"Consider the ravens: they neither sow nor reap, they have neither storehouse nor barn, and yet God feeds them. Of how much more value are you...! And can any of you by worrying add a single hour to your span of life? If then you are not able to do so small a thing as that, why do you worry about the rest?" (Luke 12:24–26)

Petitions

Where there is hatred, let me sow love, we pray.
Response: Lord, make me an instrument of peace.
Where there is injury, pardon, we pray.
Where there is doubt, faith, we pray.
Where there is despair, hope, we pray.
Where there is sadness, joy, we pray.
Where there is darkness, light, we pray.

Collect

Divine Master, grant that I may not so much seek to be consoled as to console, to be understood as to understand, to be loved as to love, for it is in giving that we receive, it is in pardoning that we are pardoned and it is in dying that we are born to eternal life.

Sharing of the Blessing Cup
Pray together the Our Father, or sing "All Creatures of Our God and King" or another appropriate song.

ON HALLOWEEN/ALL SAINTS

Opening Prayer

We celebrate a holy evening and all the saints who have gone before us in the name of the Father, and of the Son, and of the Holy Spirit.

Scripture

... you are no longer strangers... you are citizens with the saints and also members of the household of God. (Ephesians 2:19)

Petitions

Holy women and men who are models for our own Christian way of life...
Response: Pray for us.
All angels and patrons...
Family and friends who share the everlasting kingdom...
For safety and protection of the saints for children everywhere...
Add your own petitions.

Collect

May all rejoice in this kingdom on earth and in heaven, for in this cup we find unity and joy.

Sharing of the Blessing Cup

As each person receives the blessing cup, ask him or her to recount the story of the holy men and women—saints—in his or her life.

Thanksgiving Day

Opening Prayer

In the spirit of humble praise we give thanks, in the name of the Father, and of the Son, and of the Holy Spirit.

Scripture

Praise the LORD!

O give thanks to the LORD, for he is good;
for his steadfast love endures forever.
Who can utter the mighty doings of the LORD,
or declare all his praise? (Psalm 106:1–2)

Petitions

For our family, friends, relatives and those who teach us God's way, we pray.
Response: We thank you, Lord.
For our home and for the many things you surround us with in goodness, we pray.
For all creation, for sights and sounds and all our senses, we pray.
Add your own petitions.

Collect

We lift up this cup to our God with gratitude for all the gifts showered on God's people.

Sharing of the Blessing Cup
Join hands and pray together the Our Father.

Blessing of the Advent Wreath

Opening Prayer

Celebrating the endless circle of God's care, we join together on this First Sunday of Advent to light our Advent wreath and share our cup of blessing, in the name of the Father, and of the Son, and of the Holy Spirit.

Scripture

Have you not known? Have you not heard?
> Has it not been told you from the beginning?
> Have you not understood from the foundations of the earth?

It is [God] who sits above the circle of the earth...
(Isaiah 40:21–22a)

Petitions

We light this Advent candle while we await the coming of Christ our Light, and we pray.
Response: Come, Lord Jesus.
Be with us, Lord, as we prepare to celebrate the joyful feast of all God's children, we pray.
Gather us, Lord, into the circle of your love, we pray.
Add your own petitions.

Collect

As this wreath remains ever green and ever alive and our Advent candles mark the weeks until the birth of Christ, nurture in us joyful hope and expectation.

Sharing of the Blessing Cup

Pray together the Hail Mary or sing "O Come, O Come, Emmanuel."

BLESSING OF THE TREE AND CRIB

Opening Prayer

With joyful anticipation, we decorate our home and make ready our hearts for the birth of our Savior, in the name of the Father, and of the Son, and of the Holy Spirit.

Scripture

So [the shepherds] went with haste and found Mary and Joseph, and the child lying in the manger. When they saw this, they made known what had been told them about this child; and all who heard it were amazed at what the shepherds told them. (Luke 2:16–18)

Petitions

In the spirit of joy we await the celebration of Jesus' birth, and so we pray.
Response: Lord Jesus, come to us.
Make holy these evergreens that announce your ever-present love for us, we pray.
May the brightness and beauty of this tree announce the shining presence of your love, we pray.
May our Christmas manger be a reminder that our hearts are home for the Savior, we pray.
Add your own petitions.

Collect

As we anticipate the feast of Christmas, help us to keep our energies focused on you, the Lord of our lives.

Sharing of the Blessing Cup

Pray together the Our Father or the Hail Mary, or sing a Christmas song, such as "O Christmas Tree" or "Away in a Manger" or "Angels We Have Heard on High."

ADVENT SERVICE

Opening Prayer

As we prepare for the coming of the Lord, we pray in the name of the Father, and of the Son, and of the Holy Spirit.

Scripture

Now the birth of Jesus the Messiah took place in this way. When his mother Mary had been engaged to Joseph, but before they lived together, she was found to be with child from the Holy Spirit. Her husband Joseph, being a righteous man and unwilling to expose her to public disgrace, planned to dismiss her quietly. But just when he had resolved to do this, an angel of the Lord appeared to him in a dream and said, "Joseph, son of David, do not be afraid to take Mary as your wife, for the child conceived in her is from the Holy Spirit. She will bear a son, and you are to name him Jesus, for he will save his people from their sins." (Matthew 1:18–21)

Petitions

Help us to make room in our hearts for you, Lord, we pray.
Response: We wait for you, Lord.
Help us to proclaim your coming, Lord, we pray.
Help us to live in your love, Lord, we pray.
Add your own petitions.

Collect

Lord, help us to step out in faith and with openness to your will. Make us ready to greet you with peace-filled hearts.

Sharing of the Blessing Cup

Pray together the Our Father or sing an Advent song.

FOR SAINT NICHOLAS (DECEMBER 6)

Opening Prayer

As we enter into this wonderful season and celebration we joyfully begin in the name of the Father, and of the Son, and of the Holy Spirit.

Scripture

For thus says the Lord GOD: I myself will search for my sheep, and will seek them out. As shepherds seek out their flocks when they are among their scattered sheep, so I will seek out my sheep. (Ezekiel 34:11–12)

A member may want to tell the story of Saint Nicholas.

Petitions

Through acts of kindness and generosity, help us to prepare for Jesus' birth, we pray.
Response: Joy to the world.
For peace, we pray.
For the homeless, we pray.
Add your own petitions.

Collect

Through the guidance of Saint Nicholas, may those who are especially close to us be drawn closer to you, Lord Jesus.

Sharing of the Blessing Cup
Pray the Our Father or sing an appropriate song.

In Praise of Mary

Opening Prayer

Today we honor our Blessed Mother in the name of the Father, and of the Son, and of the Holy Spirit.

Scripture

...the angel Gabriel was sent by God to a town in Galilee called Nazareth, to a virgin engaged to a man whose name was Joseph, of the house of David. The virgin's name was Mary. And he came to her and said, "Greetings, favored one! The Lord is with you." (Luke 1:26–28)

Litany

Hail Mary, full of grace, the Lord is with thee.
Response: Pray for us.
Blessed art thou among women and blessed is the fruit of your womb.
Holy Mary, Mother of God, pray for us sinners, now and at the hour of our death.
Add your own petitions.

Collect

Beloved mother of Jesus and our mother, hold us near to you in the prayer we offer today.

Sharing of the Blessing Cup
Sing a favorite or appropriate Marian song.

CHRISTMAS CELEBRATION

Opening Prayer

We celebrate the birth of Jesus, in the name of the Father, and of the Son, and of the Holy Spirit.

Scripture

But the angel said to [the shepherds]: "...to you is born this day in the city of David a Savior, who is the Messiah, the Lord. This will be a sign for you: you will find a child wrapped in bands of cloth and lying in a manger." And suddenly there was with the angel a multitude of the heavenly host, praising God and saying,

> "Glory to God in the highest heaven,
> and on earth peace among those whom
> he favors!" (Luke 2:10a, 11–14)

Petitions

We celebrate the great gift of God's Son, Jesus himself, and we pray.
Response: Glory to God in the highest!
May our family become more and more like the Holy Family, we pray.
May peace fill our hearts, our home and our world, we pray.
Add your own petitions.

Collect

May the happiness of this day bring new hope to the year ahead and joy to our hearts today.

Sharing of the Blessing Cup
Pray together the Our Father or the Hail Mary, or sing your favorite Christmas song.

Other resources for families and groups from St. Anthony Messenger Press:

OTHER RESOURCES FOR FAMILIES AND GROUPS FROM ST. ANTHONY MESSENGER PRESS:

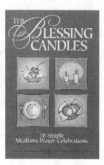

The Blessing Candles:
58 Simple Mealtime Prayer-Celebrations
By Gaynell Bordes Cronin and Jack Rathschmidt, O.F.M. Cap.

People all over the world celebrate rituals to mark solstices and equinoxes, births, personal and religious milestones, marriages, anniversaries and death. Rituals allow us to remember our past, hope for the future, live in the now and mark important events, no matter how painful, as celebrations of human becoming and faith. These prayer-rituals using two candles uncover the wonder and wisdom of faith in family or group gatherings. Each prayer-celebration includes a gathering prayer, the lighting of two candles, a reading and a prayerful response to it, reflection questions and a sending prayer.
Paper. ISBN 0-86716-379-8. $8.95

Holy Bells and Wonderful Smells: Year-round Activities for Classrooms and Families
By Jeanne Hunt

These hands-on, practical activities, designed for schoolchildren and their families, cover a wide variety of occasions: liturgical feasts, secular holidays, nature's seasons, the beginning and end of the school year, birthdays, vacations and many others. Innovative activities will spark your imagination and renew your enthusiasm for religious and secular holidays.
Paper. ISBN 0-86716-141-8. $9.95

Order from your local Catholic bookstore or:
St. Anthony Messenger Press
28 W. Liberty Street
Cincinnati, OH 45202
(513) 241-5615
1-800-488-0488 (toll-free)
www.AmericanCatholic.org